# From IDEA to BOOK

## A STEP-BY-STEP GUIDE TO WRITING YOUR BOOK IN 21 DAYS

Kirimi Barine, PhD

FROM IDEA TO BOOK: A Step-by-Step Guide to Writing Your Book in 21 Days



ISBN 978-9966-69-048-7

Published by

P.O. Box 16458 - 00100
NAIROBI. KENYA
www.publishing-institute.org
info@publishing-institute.org

# CONTENTS



WEEK **1**

WEEK **2**

WEEK **3**

# Preface

Do you dream of writing a book? Do you have a story so compelling to share with the world, but don't know how to go about becoming a published author? You are not alone. I am often approached by people who desire to write but have no idea where to begin.

Having the idea to write a book is often the easiest part of book writing. Getting to a complete manuscript can be a challenging task. Writing is often a solitary exercise. When you write, you work alone. Feelings of doubt could cloud your writing, and often, words of encouragement and advice to keep moving forward are necessary. It is also not uncommon to get stuck or experience what we commonly know as writer's block. I know how overwhelming that feeling can be. My experience of over two decades working with writers, and being an author myself, has taught me that the writing life can be lonely, and navigating the publishing process can feel like a daunting task.

However, the joy of seeing never published before authors excited about their completed projects keeps me motivated to work with budding writers.

This resource will help you overcome your writing challenges and provide the accountability and support you need to get your idea to a book.

Kirimi Barine, PhD

# HOW TO USE THIS BOOK

This book can be used for individual writing journey or in an accountability writing group setting.

To help you make the best use of the content, I have divided the book into four parts and provided space for you to write down your reflections.

Part 1 will guide you through a process of understanding the writing process with daily insights to learn from.

Part 2 provides you with reflection questions to help you apply what you have discovered from the insights read each day.

Part 3 invites you to consider the actions you will take as a result of your reading and reflection.

Part 4 provides you with a checklist for accountability to yourself.

# The Writer's Mindset

*Everything in life starts with your mindset first and your actions second. Your actions follow your thoughts, your beliefs and ideas. To make a shift, to free your energy start with getting your mind right, and then, take action.*

Sylvester Mcnutt III

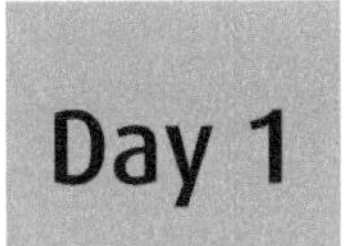

# Establish Your 'Why' for Writing Your Book

*Writing is my way of expressing—and thereby eliminating—all the various ways we can be wrong-headed.*

Zadie Smith

*I just knew there were stories I wanted to tell.*

Octavia E. Butler

Your journey to book writing begins now. Welcome! Expect to have fun and achieve accelerated results if you maintain the pace for all the 21-days.

Writing a book is not easy; it takes hard work and dedication. You will need to put in long hours, late nights, and even weekends to get it done. It may also mean deferring social engagements or other such activities until your manuscript is complete. This is why you need to be clear about why you are writing your book. When things get tough and you are tempted to give up, you will need a good reason to keep going. A solid purpose for writing the book will carry you through the challenges you may encounter during the book writing process.

Some good reasons why you may want to write a book include:

- **Building your credibility:** If you are a professional in any field, writing a book allows you to present yourself to your audience as an expert.

- **For social awareness:** Is there something you feel strongly about that you want to share with the world? Writing a book is a great way to share your thoughts.

- **To motivate and inspire:** You may desire to encourage your audience to make certain important changes as a means of improving their lives.

- **To equip and empower:** To help your audience develop a skill or better understand a certain area of expertise. This could be anything from baking, mountain climbing, puppy training, or parenting.

- **As a source of income:** You may be looking forward to the book sales as an extra source of income.

These are just examples. Your 'why' for writing a book should be personal and unique. Only make sure it's the sort of 'why' that keeps you going until your book is in the hands of your readers.

You also need to carefully consider your expectations. Many authors grapple with unrealistic expectations. For instance, if you expect that writing a book will make you famous, you are likely setting yourself up for some major disappointment.

Think about it. How many famous authors do you know who got famous purely for writing? The honest answer is: very few. Typically, people get famous in other ways, and then they write a book. Even Shakespeare became famous after his death. A more realistic expectation would be writing a book will increase your visibility and help you grow your network.

### It's time to reflect!

- What is your 'why' for writing a book? Is it compelling, and will it keep you going when other things demand your attention?

- What are your expectations once the book is complete? Are they realistic?

_________________________________________________

_________________________________________________

_________________________________________________

_________________________________________________

_________________________________________________

_________________________________________________

_________________________________________________

_________________________________________________

_________________________________________________

Share your reflections with a partner or writer's group.

## Writing Checklist

**Did I...**

- [ ] Read Day 1 Insights
- [ ] Write my reflection from today's reading
- [ ] Write my action plan
- [ ] Share my action plan for accountability with a partner or a writer's group

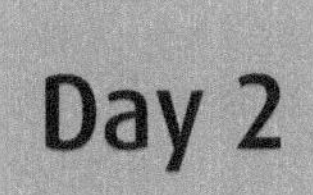

# Deal With Your Excuses for Not Writing

*It is better to offer no excuse than a bad one.*
George Washington

*He that is good for making excuses is seldom good for anything else.*
Benjamin Franklin

You've jumped over the hurdle of figuring out your 'why' of writing your book, well done! Your reason for writing will help you stay focused.

What next?

As any honest writer will tell you, your greatest obstacle to completing your book will be your own inner struggles. Plato put it this way: *Self-conquest is the greatest of victories.*

If you are like most authors, you've thought about writing a book for quite some time now but just never got round to it. Why? Well, because we all have our excuses for not getting started on our book-writing journeys. Here are some of the most common ones:

## I'm too busy

This is a good one, because it is actually true. We're all busy. However, if you examine your day, you'll find that you often find time for lots of non-essential activities. Are you able to squeeze in time for TV, social media, Internet or socialising to your busy schedule? If so, then you can devote just 30 minutes of your day to write. In fact, writing for 10 minutes twice a day will see you complete your book in no time.

## I don't have an original idea

This excuse is probably responsible for thousands, if not millions of books that have not been written. What most prospective authors don't realise is that a completely original idea would be difficult to come by for most people.

What you are likely to deliver to your audience, in most cases, is a fresh perspective on how to make an old idea work for them. A fresh perspective that is practical and applicable to your readers' situation is a great reason to get started on your book.

# I'm going to expose my ignorance

You can always trust your ego to get in the way of you sharing what's in your heart.

Many authors attach their identity to their book's success. So if it's a failure, it could affect them significantly at a personal level. If you are a professional, for example, writing a bad book could negatively affect your brand. I know writers who have walked away at the point of publishing after putting in hundreds of hours and loads of money into their book.

If you are dealing with this fear, turn your focus on the benefits of writing your book instead. How many people will miss out on the great ideas you have to share if you don't write it? What opportunities for growth will you deny yourself by walking away?

Rather than allowing fear to debilitate you, use it to motivate you to deliver a high-quality book. And get all the help you need to make sure of this, because help is available.

## It's time to reflect!

- What are your greatest fears when it comes to writing your book?
- Are your fears rational, or largely emotional?
- How can you address these fears in a positive way?

_______________________________________________

_______________________________________________

_______________________________________________

_______________________________________________

_______________________________________________

_______________________________________________

_______________________________________________

Share your reflections with a partner or a group.

As human beings, we tend to be objective about other people's issues but subjective about our own. So,your objective view may just be what a fellow author needs to overcome their fear, so feel free to engage.

## Writing Checklist

**Did I...**

- [ ] Read Day 2 Insights
- [ ] Write my reflection from today's reading
- [ ] Write my action plan
- [ ] Share my action plan for accountability with a partner or a writer's group

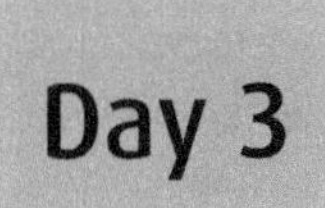

# Prepare Your Mind for the Journey

*Nothing is impossible. The word itself says I'M Possible.*

Audrey Hepburn

This quote should remind us that 'impossible' is just a label for things we just don't know how to do yet or haven't tried to do. And I am here, together with the group to help your book idea move from IMPOSSIBLE to I'M POSSIBLE.

Now that you've hopefully dealt with your excuses for not writing, the next thing to do is get your mind on board. Just like you don't prepare a meal by placing the cooking pot on the fire first, your mind needs to be prepared in advance before any writing begins. One ingredient for a successful book-writing journey is your mind.

Israelmore Ayivor rightly said, *Prior preparation is success divided by half. Once you have fully prepared, every hand glove that obstacles wear to pull you away from reaching your destination will become slippery!*

An important step in preparing your mind is to set realistic expectations. Expectations are the major ingredients for disappointment. When they are unmet, you might easily give up on the journey. Examples of issues you should prepare to deal with include:

## It's not going to be easy

Writing a book is not a walk in the park. No one ever slept and woke up to a finished manuscript. Anyone who claims to have an easy time writing a book probably didn't do a good job.

You'll need to accept that you're getting into a task that will require your best efforts. You will need to put in long hours to write and go over your work several times. You may not get encouraging words from your editor. But this shouldn't stop you because your efforts will ultimately pay off—if you keep at it.

## It may get confusing sometimes

It is common to think you should have written your book differently. For instance, you might at some point feel you ought to change the order of the chapters. Other times, it could be you feel you should have included more information. You will want to change your book title several times. All these changes may make you feel confused. However, instead of getting discouraged, encourage yourself that it shows you are really putting in the effort.

## It may get you emotionally involved

Confusion can unnerve you emotionally. You may feel anxious, wonder whether you'll ever finish your book, or feel uncertain about the quality of your finished work. At other times, fear of the unknown, of failure, etc., may grip you. Preparing for such emotional reactions beforehand will ensure they don't paralyse you.

## It's going to be tiring and/or overwhelming

Writing experts predict that when you are writing a book the right way, you will feel tired. Why? You will need to use your brain and mull over ideas. This will sometimes make you feel exhausted.

Also, as your writing progresses, you may get tired of the hours you need to put in. This means you need to plan how you will refresh and rejuvenate yourself to keep the writing momentum going.

> **It's time to reflect!**
>
> - What other factors can you think of that you should be conscious of before starting to write your book?
> - How will you overcome these challenges?

Share your reflections with a partner or a writer's group.

Develop effective plans for dealing with challenges during your individual book-writing journey.

## Writing Checklist

**Did I...**

- [ ] Read Day 3 notes
- [ ] Write my reflection from today's reading
- [ ] Write my action plan
- [ ] Share my action plan for accountability with a partner or a writer's group

# Beat the Writer's Block

*If you want to change the world, pick up your pen and write.*

Martin Luther

Have you ever tried to put pen to paper (or fingers to keyboard) and frozen? Have you ever had moments when the words elude you? Do you ever doubt your ability to convey the message you have circling about your brain?

John Rogers said, *You can't think yourself out of a writing block; you have to write yourself out of a thinking block.*

The writer's block is the dreaded 'plague' with the potential of bringing your writing to a sudden halt. Learning how to overcome it in advance could very well save your book, so please don't ignore it. When you experience this phenomenon, you may feel like you've run out of all your creative juices. It usually manifests when you're at your desk, and your mind suddenly goes 'blank' and you have nothing to write. In other instances, the exact opposite happens and you feel you have so many important things you feel you need to put down, to the extent that you are unable to write anything.

Here are some tips to deal with the writer's block:

## Refer to your bigger picture

A quick glance at your writing plan may be all you need to trigger fresh thoughts. Run a mental jog back and forth on your outline. Remind yourself what you had intended to write about and try to recapture your thought pattern.

Referring back to your outline regularly is actually highly recommended. Seeing the big picture and then getting back to your current position will often give you a jumpstart. Moreover, it will keep you focused and on-topic as you keep moving toward your desired end.

## Make a change

The English proverb states that 'a change is as good as a rest'. As you plan to write, it may really help to have more than one location for writing. Also, select different ways of writing. For example, you can switch between your laptop and tablet, or keep your regular writing pad close so you can write by hand when the mood calls for it.

A change of location or device may be all you need to keep the flow of writing going. Part of changing your environment includes adding some incentives to your writing. If music helps you relax, for example, you can have different playlists with instrumental music on stand-by.

## Take healthy breaks

Making changes should not replace actual breaks. The human body is very interesting in how it works. Exercise, in particular, is one energy booster you don't want to miss out on. It releases 'feel-good' hormones that could just be the solution to your writing paralysis. You can fit your exercise regimen in between your writing sessions, or at other strategic times.

## Have a conversation

Talking about what you are writing about can help you get past the 'blankness'. This could be a conversation with yourself or a friend. Getting someone who can ask you questions can really prove to be helpful. It could also give you new ideas to include in your writing, just remember to stay on-topic.

## Look at what you've already written

Seeing what you've already accomplished may be the push you need to keep going. It will also help you identify areas or ideas you probably didn't exhaust. However, remember to put off editing until the first draft is complete.

- What do you usually do to improve your mood whenever you are down or discouraged?

- How many people can you think of who you could engage in meaningful conversation about your topic of interest? Write their names.

- Are there other authors you respect who have written on your subject area and might help trigger new thoughts for your book? Write their names.

- What other methods of overcoming writer's block do you think might be effective for you?

Share your reflections with a partner or a group.

Remember, writer's block is bound to occur. Get your ammunition ready to overcome it.

## Writing Checklist

**Did I...**

- [ ] Read Day 4 Insights
- [ ] Write my reflection from today's reading
- [ ] Write my action plan
- [ ] Share my action plan for accountability with a partner or a writer's group

# Watch Out for Three Writer 'Potholes'

*Stop worrying about the potholes in the road and enjoy the journey.*

Babs Hoffman

We've already established the fact that the book-writing process has its difficulties. That's why you don't want to make it any harder than it needs to be. Unfortunately, many writers experience more difficulties than they need to, because they are unaware of certain common writing potholes.

The good thing is, like anything in life, knowing the traps that you might fall into before your journey begins allows you to avoid them, or it at least helps you mentally prepare to deal with them. Here are 3 major potholes you should watch out for:

## Editing while you write

Most writers I know suffer from some form of perfectionism. I say 'suffer' in regard to the negative effect it could have in your writing journey. Striving to do the best you can is certainly a good thing, but it's not so great when the need to perfect your book gets you stuck on the first chapter.

Remember, the first draft is not meant to be perfect. In fact, your goal when writing your first draft is to put what's in your head on paper, which is a big enough hurdle. No need to complicate it.

Another reason why you shouldn't edit while you write is because these two processes use different parts of your brain. The writing process uses the creative parts while editing uses the critical parts. Once you get into a critical frame of mind, it's very difficult to go back to pure creativity again.

## Delaying the formatting process

Poor formatting is a sure turn-off for readers, so you want to get it right from the very start. Writers should also note that formatting can prove difficult when you already have your content written. It's always better to think about and plan your formatting before you start to write. It will save you a lot of time and trouble.

As you start to write, ensure that your sentences and paragraphs are aligned properly. Remember to distribute sub-headings appropriately. Tools like Microsoft Word allow you to format your document as you write, so consider this when selecting the most appropriate tool.

## Procrastination

If there's a common malady that virtually all writers face, it's procrastination. This is why a writing plan is essential for writing success. A plan breaks down your writing into actionable steps that won't overwhelm you.

But what if you already have a plan, but still find yourself procrastinating? If you're like most people, you'll probably castigate yourself for being lazy and undisciplined. However, procrastination may be a legitimate hesitation to start writing.

For instance, you may not feel confident about your writing plan. If that's the case, then go over your plan again and tweak it accordingly. Is this your first book? Then you may feel intimidated. But like we already discussed, there are ways to evaluate and work through your fears or misgivings about writing.

Sometimes you just need a break; take a walk and then get back to your writing. Sometimes you just need some motivation; call up a friend and get that pep talk. And sometimes, you just need to remind yourself that there's no such thing as the perfect writer.

For you to write and do it well, don't try to be your own editor designer, and proofreader of your book. Allow experts to support you. Your duty is to communicate the message as clearly as you can and where you can't do it, get support to help you make it meaningful to your audience. So, when you start writing, just write and write.

- What other 'potholes' do you think a writer might struggle with?

- What specific steps will you take to ensure you get the formatting process for your book right?

- What might be your biggest reason for procrastinating when writing your book?

___________________________________________

___________________________________________

___________________________________________

___________________________________________

___________________________________________

___________________________________________

___________________________________________

___________________________________________

___________________________________________

___________________________________________

___________________________________________

___________________________________________

Share your reflections with a partner or a group.

## Writing Checklist

**Did I...**

- [ ] Read Day 5 Insights
- [ ] Write my reflection from today's reading
- [ ] Write my action plan
- [ ] Share my action plan for accountability with a partner or a writer's group

# THE WRITER'S ENVIRONMENT:

*Create positive space around you,even if it's in your min.You must have an environment of good energy ,in order to give that.*

https://quotesgram.com/

 # Schedule Your Writing Time

*There are no secrets to success. It is the result of preparation, hard work, and learning from failure.*

Colin Powell

So far, you've already taken up a writer's mindset. Congratulations! You can now begin to prepare to write. As we saw earlier, you can't will your book into existence. You must create a plan.

One of the primary ways to plan for writing is to determine when you will be writing. No, you cannot limit your writing to whenever you feel like it. In fact, waiting to feel inspired is a sure-fire way to never finish your book. It is also not about 'finding time' for writing. You will need to create time, that is, block out time to write.

How do you do this?

## Critically analyse your daily schedule

You are the author. You are the one putting pen to paper. This means you will have to invest your time if you are to complete your book-writing project. Take a keen look at your schedule. How do you spend your 24 hours?

Hopefully, you have a regular schedule. If you don't, you can outline the general activities that require your attention each day. If you are honest with yourself, you will see your pattern and identify a time slot you can set aside for writing.

## Knock out the non-essentials

Okay, you need to face it. There are activities in your day you can do without. You probably don't think so now, but a careful look at your day will reveal otherwise. How can you do this?

Try having an alarm at the top of every hour and when it goes off, ask yourself how you have spent that hour. You'll be surprised at how many minutes fly past and you cannot account for them. Ask yourself what activities take up your time, and which ones you can do without.

As you do this, avoid the temptation to gnaw away at family time.

# Consider your most fruitful times

Each person is different. Are you an early riser? Are you a night owl? Or do you always find yourself looking for an 'escape' from your daily routine? This may just be your best writing opportunity if you take it seriously.

Whatever works for you, ensure you choose a time when you can produce quality work. Of course, this doesn't mean that your work must be perfect. It just means you've chosen a time when you are most likely to write your best.

In addition, make it your policy to write daily. *Consistency is the secret to successful book writing.*

# Be realistic

Ensure you do not set unrealistic writing schedules. Being realistic means not setting targets that are too high or thinking the time you can set aside is too little. For example, it would be crazy to expect yourself to write for five hours every day and be consistent. Many writers oscillate between 30 minutes and three hours of writing on a single day. Remember, even 10 minutes each day will be better than nothing.

It is also important to set an actual time, say at 0700-0730hrs daily. Be specific.



- What non-essential activities can you eliminate from your schedule to create time for book writing?
- How can you adjust your day to ensure your most fruitful time is not lost?

____________________________________________________

____________________________________________________

____________________________________________________

____________________________________________________

____________________________________________________

✎ Once you're done, share your reflections with a friend or writing partner. You might discover your blind spots as you get new insights.

✎ Keep engaging!

## Writing Checklist

**Did I...**

☐ Read Day 6 Insights

☐ Write my reflection from today's reading

☐ Write my action plan

☐ Share my action plan for accountability with a partner or a writer's group

# Develop Your Writing Habit (Part 1)

**Day 7**

*Habits are formed by the repetition of particular acts. They are strengthened by an increase in the number of repeated acts. Habits are also weakened or broken, and contrary habits are formed by the repetition of contrary acts.*

Mortimer Adler

*Your beliefs become your thoughts,*
*Your thoughts become your words,*
*Your words become your actions,*
*Your actions become your habits,*
*Your habits become your values,*
*Your values become your destiny.*

Mahatma Gandhi

Repeat the actions you want to reinforce and they will become your habits.

Once you have determined your best writing time and gone ahead to block it out, the next hurdle to jump is developing your writing habits. This is what Warren Buffet says, 'Chains of habit are too light to be felt until they are too heavy to be broken.' Once you work out your writing habit, it'll almost come naturally to go to your writing space and make progress. For that to happen, you may need to:

## Consult

One way to do this, especially if this is your first time writing a book, is to get ideas from other authors. After all, you don't want to waste precious time reinventing the wheel. You will do well to equip yourself with sound advice at the onset.

Find out how you can manage your time. Ask them what they did to beat their deadlines and stay focused throughout the project. Then pick what works for you. If you don't know an author personally, do a quick search online and you'll find plenty of advice waiting for you.

# Maintain a progress report

There is nothing as encouraging as observing your own progress. It could be as simple as tallying the days you write consistently on the calendar. You could also use an app. Just remember that habit is formed by doing something continuously.

For starters, consider setting the 21-day mark as your target. Specialists say that habits are formed after consistently doing something for 3 weeks straight. You may want to start on this immediately, so that by the time you start writing, you're already headed towards forming a habit.

# Report your progress to someone

Writing is not a journey you want to take alone. There will be times when you are sure you want to give up. If you don't find an accountability partner to give a report on your progress, you'll quickly find it difficult to stay on track.

Even though you count yourself as a self-driven individual, an accountability partner reminds you stick to the plan. You may not appreciate this when all your creative juices are at optimum level; but when things get tough and you need to put in the extra effort to keep going, you will see the benefit. Reporting your progress to someone could be just what saves your book-writing dream from a premature death.

It is critical that you choose the right person to whom you will give your progress report. It needs to be someone who:

- Has your respect

- Has your back

- Is committed to seeing you succeed

- Will not allow you to give up

- Will tell you the hard truth every time

- Knows what works for you and gets you to do it

This person could be a friend, a mentor or perhaps a fellow author. If you get a person who is all the three, the better for you! If not, you can choose a person who is also planning to write a book. Peer motivation is a great incentive and can help you both to remain faithful.

- Who can you consult concerning your book-writing habits? Write their name(s) and why you think they would be helpful to you.

- How do you plan to keep track of your progress?

- Write a list of people you can give a report on your writing schedule. Why do you think this is important?

Share your reflections with a partner or a writer's group.

Remember, your writing habit will get you to the finish line, start developing a healthy one today!

## Writing Checklist

**Did I...**

- [ ] Read Day 7 Insights
- [ ] Write my reflection from today's reading
- [ ] Write my action plan
- [ ] Share my action plan for accountability with a partner or a writer's group

# Develop and Writing Habits (Part 2)

*I have learned that champions aren't just born; champions can be made when they embrace and commit to life-changing positive habits.*

Lewis Howes

*You'll never change your life until you change something you do daily. The secret of your success is found in your daily routine.*

John Maxwell

I couldn't agree more with Lewis Howes. Authors aren't just born; they can be made when they embrace and commit to write-changing habits. If you are reading this book, you are on your way to being made an author. Ignite your potential and be the best author you can be.

At this point, you have already discovered some of the resourceful people who might give you valid ideas on creating useful writing habits. You have also considered some ways you will track your progress. Finally, you have names of individuals you will commit to give regular reports on your writing progress. You are doing great; you deserve a pat on the back.

Did you know other facets of your life affect your writing? Consider an athlete like Eliud Kipchoge, who won the INEOS 1:59 Challenge. He had to ensure every aspect of his life contributed positively toward his goal. That included his diet, sleep, daily exercise, and training.

As an author, you also need to think about the daily habits that will help your writing goal succeed.

## Physical health habits

You need to be healthy throughout your writing project if you're going to make it to the finish line. If you don't have an exercise plan that you follow every week, I recommend picking one today. Not only will it keep your body healthy, it will refresh your mind too.

Remember, exervcise doesn't have to be complicated. Simply go with what you love. Walking, jogging, skipping, or swimming could be just what you need to keep your body in optimum health.

# Routine habits

As much as you would love to have a disciplined writing habit, this could easily take a fatal blow if the rest of your life is disorderly. How do you get a working daily routine? It isn't rocket science.

If you have a job, you are already at a head start. Even if you're a stay-at-home parent, your chores are your job and will force you to organise your time. Sticking to a regular pattern of keeping up with other daily activities will help you stick to your writing schedule as well.

# Focus-boosting habits

This is just a fancy way of saying that you need to learn how to deal with distractions. If you are the kind of person who easily ends up doing things you hadn't intended to do (which is most of us, if we're being honest), this is a big one for you.

Determine how you will avoid distractions. Learn to say no. Make a plan and stick to it, no matter how tempted you are to do otherwise. Switch of your phone or TV. Whatever it takes, learn to say no to stuff that could subtly steal your time.

# Researching habits

To be a good writer, you need to develop a habit of regular research. I know this may put you off, especially if you don't consider yourself much of a scholar. However, research is not limited to the world of academia.

Whenever you read a book, look at how the author presents their ideas. Do the same when you watch TV or any movie. Ask yourself how the content creators keep their audiences glued to the screens. You can learn some tips from their styles of communication.

# Celebration habits

This is very important for you to cultivate. If you're the kind of person who is often too hard on yourself, you need to drop that attitude. Learn to celebrate yourself. Daily!

Recognise your own efforts and give yourself rewards when you hit milestones. This might just turn out to be a very effective way of keeping yourself going. Before you know it, you'll be at the finish line.

[1] https://www.ted.com/talks/tim_urban_inside_the_mind_of_a_master_procrastinator

- Do you already have a way to maintain your physical health? If not, what exercise plan can you adopt from today?

- What can you do to ensure your daily schedule is more organised?

- What are the common distractors you find yourself dealing with daily? How do you plan to say no to them?

- Are you a good researcher? Why do you think so (or not) and how can you improve?

- Do you celebrate yourself enough? How? And if not, in what ways can you begin to do this?

Share your reflections with tyour friend or writing partner.

Your writing habits won't exist in a bubble, so focus on transforming your life in meaningful ways!

## Writing Checklist

**Did I...**

- [ ] Read Day 8 Insights
- [ ] Write my reflection from today's reading
- [ ] Write my action plan
- [ ] Share my action plan for accountability with a partner or a writer's group

# Set Deadlines

*Goals are dreams with **deadlines.***

*- Napoleon Hill*

Deadlines are simply essential for writers. They help you prioritise and remain focused and avoid procrastination. Tim Urban has some good lessons on procrastination. See his TED Talk video[1].

One of the major ways to keep yourself on track and moving toward your goal of completing your book is to set a deadline. A deadline plays the crucial role of helping you stick to your schedule so you can complete your manuscript on time. Some things to consider as you set your deadlines include:

## How long should the book be?

Are you asking how you can set a deadline when you don't know how long you actually need to write the book? Good question. The general rule of thumb is one month for a book of 30,000 words. This roughly translates to 1000 words per day. So, if you write 500 words each day, your deadline would be two months.

Let me point out here that the ideal word count varies depending on your genre and your target audience. This means that you should first determine your word count then divide it by your daily target to get to your deadline date. It is, therefore, important to research on the ideal word count for the sort of book you want to write.

## Your writing calendar

A simple printed monthly calendar should suffice when setting your schedule. Start by marking off the days when you know you won't be able to write at all. Then, based on the number of days you've already determined you need to complete your first draft, you can set a date that actually works.

Once you've set your deadline, be sure to share it with your identified accountability partner. Working with an editor also helps, and is in fact highly recommended. Your deadline can be the date when you commit to deliver your first draft to your editor.

In addition to having a deadline for when you'll complete your book, also set deadlines for smaller milestones. Create a schedule for when the first draft of chapter 1 will be done, chapter 2, and so forth. Ensure your deadlines are reasonable and based on how much you can do each day. Setting unrealistic goals will only eat away at your morale as you keep missing each milestone.

Something else that will push you to stay accountable is to announce to your friends and family that you are writing a book. You'll likely get a lot of positive feedback, which is great for morale when starting out. It will also help you keep pushing yourself whenever you are tempted to slack off.

## Other important activities

We've focused on the deadlines for the actual writing because it is the activity you have the most control over. However, you will also need to set deadlines for other activities that count towards the final book, not just the actual writing. These include preparing your outline, doing your research, editing, and publishing.

Setting deadlines for these additional activities helps you have a goal with which to work. Of course, it is important to be flexible with these deadlines, because the activities could take more or less time than you expect as you learn what your personal writing process looks like.

> **It's time to reflect!**
>
> - What's your rough estimate for how much time it will take you to complete your book?
>
> - What do you think would be your greatest challenge in terms of beating your deadlines?
>
> - What will guide you when establishing a time estimate for activities like research, editing, and publishing?

_______________________________________________

_______________________________________________

_______________________________________________

_______________________________________________

Share your reflections with a partner or a writer's group.

## Writing Checklist

**Did I...**

- [ ] Read Day 9 Insights
- [ ] Write my reflection from today's reading
- [ ] Write my action plan
- [ ] Share my action plan for accountability with a partner or a writer's group

<table><tr><td>Day 10</td><td>Create Your Space</td></tr></table>

# Day 10 — Create Your Space

*Progress is impossible without change, and those who cannot change their minds cannot change anything.*

George Bernard Shaw

'Real writers' don't wait for inspiration to strike. Instead, they produce a set number of words or pages on a regular schedule. The first step is to find the things that trigger your creative state. Creativity is different for everyone. Some writers love working in a bustling, crowded café; others work best in a quiet room or at a retreat venue by the beach or green space.

Every professional has a territory where he or she exercises his or her skills. For a surgeon, it's the theatre. For a swimmer, it's the pool. For a chef, it's the kitchen. For an author, it's their writing space. For these other professionals, once they get into their territory, there is a mental shift. For writers, it's often their writing space that needs the shift into writing mode.

Setting aside a specific place to write is very essential. It will trigger your brain into action! This, however, doesn't have to get you all worked up. You don't need to hire space to do your writing. Work with what you have. Here are some suggestions you may want to consider:

## Serene location

If you can get a place that can get you away from all the noise around you, you're good to go. Ideally, this should be a space you can control. That is, you get to determine how it looks and what goes into it. You should also have easy access to it at your dedicated writing time.

This isn't always possible though. If you live with other people, it may be difficult to get that 'quiet' place. Try to get headphones that block out the noise or choose a writing time when there is little to no activity around you. This time could become your space. If you love the outdoors, there's nothing wrong with making the park your writing space.

# Inspirational items

These are things that activate your mind and encourage creativity. If you have a writing room, put a painting on the wall if you love art. Perhaps you love nature, but can't write from outside. Consider having some potted plants in your writing room. For someone else, photos of people they love could just be the inspiration they need.

Whatever you do, add something that will create the comfortable environment that allows you to write. If your space isn't entirely yours, like a library, carry an item that will make it feel more familiar.

# Comfortable chair

This may seem obvious, but it is often taken for granted. Ensure your body is comfortable. This can be a major cause of derailment at the subconscious level. If your body struggles or is exposed to discomfort, it will rebel without your permission.

If you have any physical challenge, you need to pay more attention to this. Your comfort is of great importance. It will also prevent further physical complications.

# Internet-free

Believe it or not, you'll do well to block out the Internet in your writing space. There are tons of stuff competing for your attention on the Internet. To avoid any contradiction, writing time shouldn't turn into 'research time'. Avoid the temptation to use that as an excuse.

Nothing could be more disappointing than realising your dedicated time has been wasted on social media. Plus, the fact that you can't relive any moment should encourage you to make the most of the time you have.

- Describe your perfect writing space.

- What other items, apart from a chair, do you consider necessary for your writing experience to be more comfortable?

Once you are done jotting down your answers, share your reflections with a friend or a group.

Remember, you are an author, and just like any other professional, you need your territory.

## Writing Checklist

**Did I...**

- [ ] Read Day 10 Insights
- [ ] Write my reflection from today's reading
- [ ] Write my action plan
- [ ] Share my action plan for accountability with a partner or a writer's group

# THE WRITER'S TOOLS & WRITING PROCESS

*A good tool improves the way you work. A great tool improves the way you think.*

Jeff Duntemann

<table><tr><td>Day 11</td><td># Identify the Writing Tools for You</td></tr></table>

*Man is a tool-using animal. Nowhere do you find him without tools; without tools he is nothing, with tools he is all.*

Thomas Carlyle

You have heard it said, *the bad workman always blames his tools*. Our success or failure is determined not by what we have to work with but by how we use what we have. A good workman finds the right tools for his or her work.

Just like a chef requires several utensils to aid in the cooking process, you, as an author, need certain writing tools. Your choice on the tool to use will depend on your preferences and access. However, this is not possible if you don't know your options. Finding the right tools can make writing productive and satisfying.

While some of the tools may be available for free, there are others that require a subscription.

## Writing and organising your content

### Notebook and Pen

Don't underestimate the power of a simple notebook. You never know when inspiration will strike next, so it's best to be prepared. Notebooks are portable, durable, stylish, and perfect for jotting down brilliant ideas.

### Microsoft Word

As one of the early word processors, Microsoft Word probably has the most variety in formatting options. If you need to write a longer document with many sections or headers, Word has you covered.

### Google Docs

Google Docs is great for collaboration. It allows you to invite others to make suggestions and comment on your work. I highly recommend this.

*Scrivener*

This app allows you to view your notes, research, outline, and writing all in one place. It allows chapter view, can create daily word targets, and allows formatting as well.

*Evernote*

Evernote helps organise your ideas, notes, research, or any other important information you want to quickly store as you find it so you can easily access it later. It is efficient since it is a mobile app, supports note-taking anytime and everywhere. It has additional features on subscription.

# Editing

*Grammarly*

Grammarly's products do more than identify grammar and spelling mistakes; they also offer detailed writing enhancements focused on clarity, conciseness, and tone. You can install Grammarly as an extension for Chrome, Safari, or Firefox web browsers for free, or check longer pieces of writing in Grammarly's online editor. Grammarly Premium, a paid service, provides deeper writing feedback, detects plagiarism, and offers style and vocabulary enhancements.

*Pro Writing Aid*

Pro Writing Aid is a desktop app you can use with programs like Scrivener, Word, and Google Docs. It catches grammar errors, suggests style changes, and even checks for plagiarism.

# Productivity Tools

*Asana*

Asana is a web and mobile application designed to help you organise, track, and manage your work.

*Freedom*

Freedom allows you to block apps, social media, email, and whatever websites you choose—and on your own schedule.

## Twords

Twords describes itself as 'the web app that nudges you to write'. The app operates based on three principles—awareness, accountability, and consistency. Twords highlights your writing habits by tracking how much you write each day and month. 'Accountability buddies' notify you when you miss several days of writing. If you get writer's block, you can consult a library of prompts, set a timer to challenge yourself to write for a specific amount of time, or read an article about the habits of successful authors.

# Other Writing and Formatting Tools

## Vellum

Creates beautiful eBooks, eBook preview, and can also create paperback books. It allows for eBook design. It is free to use but you must pay in order to export the final work.

## Reedsy Book Editor

Formats books as you write, motivates writing through glimpses of the final look, and is available online.

This list is by no means exhaustive, but it can get you started on the search for the writing tools that would work best for you. Stay focused on crafting your book and stick with the book-writing software that gives you the best results in terms of saving you money, time, and frustration.

### It's time to reflect!

- What other writing tools do you know about that could aid your writing process?

- Which apps or software could you incorporate to help you minimise the distractions that may come along your way?

___________________________________________________________

___________________________________________________________

___________________________________________________________

___________________________________________________________

Share your reflections with a partner or a writer's group.

There's a lot you can incorporate to your list of tools. Remember, you still need to choose what works best for you based on your specific needs and circumstances.

## Writing Checklist

**Did I...**

- [ ] Read Day 11 Insights
- [ ] Write my reflection from today's reading
- [ ] Write my action plan
- [ ] Share my action plan for accountability with a partner or a writer's group

<table><tr><td>Day 12</td><td># Understand the Publishing Process</td></tr></table>

*A professional writer is an amateur who didn't quit.*

Richard Bach

Few first-time writers know what goes on behind the scenes in the publishing process. Developing a basic understanding of the publishing process with a realisation of how each stage can affect the sale of your book is crucial to your success. The more knowledge you have about the marketplace and the publishing process, the better your chance of making your publishing dreams come true.

There are two crucial parts to successful publishing: The first is the writing and completion of your manuscript and preparing it for publication, and the second is everything that goes along with the packaging, production, marketing, sale and distribution of your book. Knowing how all this comes together gives you a better chance of influencing the decisions that can make or break your book's success.

With all your writing tools in place, it's important to realise that writing, editing, and publishing are worlds apart. We've said this before; as you write, don't worry about typos. Your aim is to put all your ideas on paper. Editing along the way could kill your impetus, especially if you are prone to criticising yourself.

The publishing process transforms the raw material of your book or manuscript into the finished product. This process requires your financial investment and so it is important to understand how it goes. You will also know what to expect from a publisher, or learn what you need to do if you opt for self-publishing.

## Editing

Successful editing should be done by an objective, independent person. You cannot effectively edit your own book. You will fall to see all the areas that need attention. Editing happens at two major levels: macro and micro levels. Ensure your manuscript goes through these editing steps:

1) *Developmental editing:* This focuses on the bigger picture of the book—the main ideas. The goal here is to ensure there are no inconsistencies or repetitive thoughts.

2) *Structural editing:* This focuses on the best way to communicate. For example, including a flashback or breaking a chapter into subsections could enhance the appeal of the book.

3) *Copy editing:* This deals with all the grammar-related issues (like typos) in your text.

4) *Line editing:* This examines the style of writing to make it more creative.

5) *Proofreading:* This process pays keen attention to the finer details of the manuscript so that it is ready for printing.

In the end, your content should be clear, relevant, concise, and simple. It is preferable to do all your editing sometime after you have completed your writing process. Editing is best done through fresh eyes. That's why it is better to have someone else do it for you.

## Design and Layout

Once your manuscript is free from error and has a clear style of communication, you need to go through the formatting process. This includes inserting the page numbers, chapter titles, highlights, and margins.

You will also need to get an attractive book cover design. This is one of the stages of your book-writing journey for which I highly recommend going for professional services. You can't afford to go wrong with a book cover. This will either capture the attention of potential readers or cause them to easily dismiss it. Get the best you can afford. Although they tell us not to judge a book by its cover, the truth is, a good cover sells.

## Distribution

It goes without saying that the final copy of your book must be available for distribution. You could take several approaches to this end. For instance, if you already have some followers who are willing to read your first set of books, they could be your primary target group. Through them, you can get book reviews. They can also form part of the team that launches your book.

Another distribution channel you may want to pursue is the eBook option. This expands your reach and makes your book available to many more people. You may want to market it on online shopping sites such as Amazon.

You might also consider the print-on-demand option. This gives you the option of only printing books when you get orders for them. It helps you avoid locking your money in printed books. In the long run, you can easily make follow-up editions without worrying about selling the previous ones.

Authors are their own best marketers. Speaking engagements and training engagements provide great opportunities for book distribution.

- Do you intend to self-publish or not? What are your reasons?

- How do you intend to carry out your book distribution? Who can you consult as you make your decision? Have you been part of a launch team before? If yes, what did you learn from the process?

Share your reflections with a partner or a writer's group.

Be willing to learn and open to ideas that may be different from yours. Remember, what's worth doing is worth doing well.

## Writing Checklist

**Did I...**

- [ ] Read Day 12 Insights
- [ ] Write my reflection from today's reading
- [ ] Write my action plan
- [ ] Share my action plan for accountability with a partner or a writer's group

<table><tr><td>Day 13</td><td><h1>Do the Math</h1></td></tr></table>

*The reason many people fail is not for lack of vision but for lack of resolve and resolve is born out of counting the cost.*

Robert H. Goddard

With some clarity and understanding of the roadmap to your destination in the publishing journey, it is time to count the cost. What will it take to get your idea into a book and to someone's hands?

Now that you have understood the publishing process, it's time to put on the accountant hat. Compare your book to starting a business. Would you start a business without a plan? Wouldn't you need to establish all the costs you'll incur when starting up your business?

In the same manner, you need to consider how much it will cost you to finally get your book in the market. First, you need to have the right attitude. Shift your mind from considering your book-writing project as an expense. Instead, you need to appreciate that it is an investment.

## Time investment

Whether you choose to work with a publisher or to self-publish, your time investment goes without saying. You'll need to put in lots of hours of writing to complete the book. Depending on your schedule and discipline, you may be able to hit your deadline, be done beforehand, or go over it.

## Editing investment

You will need to factor in the costs for developmental, structural, copy and line editing, as well as the cost of proofreading.

When you are looking out for an editor or publisher, ensure you get a rough estimate for each of these costs. Again, get recommendations from people who have written before. You might also want to consider getting quotes from different service providers before you finally settle on one.

# Design investment

Design, as we discussed, includes both formatting and cover designing. Invest in high quality formatting to make your book appeal to your audience. Note that you have the option of getting separate service providers for these two roles. This makes sense, especially if you know people with specialised skills in these two areas. However, the best and most convenient option is to work with a provider that specialises in both. Do your research and compare the figures. Don't settle for anything less than the best. Remember, there are writing tools that also assist with the formatting process. This may help to lower your final investment in the design process. However, the amount of time it may take you and the quality of production may not be worth it if you are looking for a professional look and feel of the book. Besides, a number of these solutions offer basic templates that may not reflect every genre of writing.

# Distribution investment

Once all the above are done, remember that you cannot distribute your book if it doesn't have an ISBN number. This is the barcode at the back of every book. It identifies your book internationally. If you plan to have your book in different formats, such as an eBook, or as paperback, you'll need separate ISBN's for each.

If you plan to launch your book, then your budget should consider the number of copies you want in print. If you have a target group you intend to avail the first copies to, this needs to be accounted for. If you want to go into marketing the book, find out what marketing channels are available.

**It's time to reflect!**

- Which part of the publishing process do you think you will need to make the greatest investment and why?

- What additional budget items do you think might be important?

- What are some of the ways you can think of that might help finance your book-writing budget?

Share your reflections with a partner or a writer's group.

There's a lot to learn from each other. If you have questions on the subject, feel free to post them as well.

## Writing Checklist

**Did I...**

- [ ] Read Day 13 Insights
- [ ] Write my reflection from today's reading
- [ ] Write my action plan
- [ ] Share my action plan for accountability with a partner or a writer's group

<table><tr><td>Day 14</td><td># Conducting Research for Your Book</td></tr></table>

*To do the writing, I have to have time to do research.*

Jean-Jacques Annaud

Generally, research is an organised and systematic method of finding answers to questions. Before we start developing an outline and get into our writing, there are important questions we need to find answers to. Let's check them out in today's reading.

## Why research?

Different authors conduct research for their book for different reasons. Any research you conduct should contribute positively to your final product. The top reason why you should consider doing some research before writing your book is to help you build your credibility. Here's how:

- Referring to other experts will help you back up the claims you make in your book.

- Using recent statistics on your subject matter will help readers understand the relevance of your views or advice.

- It helps you ensure that any information you rely on is factual.

## What to research

It is important to establish the kind of evidence that your target audience might need in order to trust your personal views. This will help you come up with a suitable research plan that will help you stay focused. Failing to plan your research could quickly turn it into a never-ending activity, and you might never actually get down to writing your book.

Your book outline will also be a helpful resource for planning your research. This is because the outline will help you identify any knowledge gaps you need to address. Here are some questions to ask:

- What sort of experts do you want to refer to?

- What statistics would help you build your argument?

- What additional information don't you have but your readers might find useful?

# Competing authors

When carrying out your research, be careful about wanting to ensure that your book idea is new. This will take you down a rabbit trail of wanting to find out what every author before you says about your subject matter. We've already talked about this before, but it's worth repeating. Your goal should never be to write about something that's never been heard of before. On the contrary, you want to give your unique perspective on the subject matter.

At the same time, it is helpful to see what others tackling your subject matter have written. Identifying where your ideas diverge, for instance, would help you identify which areas you want to put greater emphasis on for your book. Similarly, even if you draw the same conclusions, you would know where to place more emphasis to highlight your unique viewpoint. Further, you could take advantage of their bibliographies to find relevant information sources for your book.

## It's time to reflect!

- Do you have some idea of what your book will be about? Are there any knowledge gaps you need to address using research?

- What useful considerations do you think are important when developing a research plan?

- What are some of the benefits and drawbacks you can think of that might result from focusing your research on competing authors or books?

Share your reflections with a partner or a writer's group.

While reading widely is great, it will not help you find your unique writing voice; putting pen to paper will.

## Writing Checklist

**Did I...**

- [ ] Read Day 14 Insights
- [ ] Write my reflection from today's reading
- [ ] Write my action plan
- [ ] Share my action plan for accountability with a partner or a writer's group

# Where to Conduct Research for Your Book

*Research is formalised curiosity. It is poking and prying with a purpose.*

Zora Neale Hurston

Now that we know there are important questions we need to find answers to, where do we find the information and what tools are helpful for this part of the process?

We've already covered why research is important and some of the major questions to ask yourself when conducting research for your book. We have also talked about using books by competing authors for your research, and the benefits you could gain from that.

Today, we'll discuss where to do research and the best information sources available.

## Online

The Internet has played a role in making information readily available. It can, therefore, serve as an excellent source of information. However, the Internet is probably also the biggest source of disinformation, so you need to be smart.

Whenever you're conducting research on the World Wide Web, it is important to make sure any information you rely on is from a reputable source or author. Be very careful about trusting a source too quickly, because in this age of 'fake news', there are probably more websites and authors giving inaccurate information than the reliable sources.

I recommend taking your time to establish the reliability of a website or author through some background research. If you don't know an author you want to quote, check their LinkedIn profile, for instance. Their educational and professional background is a good place to start.

## Online Research Tools

1.  Zotero is a free, easy-to-use tool to help you collect, organise, cite, and share research.

2.  Answerthepublic.com —use this website to discover what people are asking about

3.  Google.com

# Books

Another great source for information is books. These are usually much more reliable than Internet sources. Hardly would anyone put in the work and effort to write a book if all they have to offer is false information. We already discussed how looking ignorant is a major concern for most authors. Investing in a book that is likely to be debunked is not a risk rational authors are willing to take.

In fact, looking or sounding ignorant is a much bigger concern for book authors than, say, online bloggers. For one, a blogger, or website owner, can easily take down an article that's been discovered to have false information. On the other hand, once a book is out there, it will serve as evidence of the author's reliability (or lack thereof) even for future generations.

# Testimonials

Personal experiences from actual people are sometimes exactly what you need to make a compelling argument. If your book is about a different approach to doing business, include a real life example or a case study of how this has worked. You could also request an expert or specialist in your field to contribute a quotation or brief passage that you might include in your book.

**It's time to reflect!**

- Identify some of the best sources of information you might use for your book idea. Why would you go with them?

- What else might you consider when doing background research on an online information source or author?

- How would you know that you've done enough research for your book?

- What are some ways you can think of to keep your research material organised?

Share your reflections with a partner or a writer's group.

Once you start writing, you might discover you need to conduct some more research on a particular topic. Should this happen, just make a note of this, but go on writing. Again, you don't want to stop the creative process once you begin.

## Writing Checklist

**Did I...**

☐ Read Day 15 Insights

☐ Write my reflection from today's reading

☐ Write my action plan

☐ Share my action plan for accountability with a partner or a writer's group

# THE WRITER'S PREPARATION:

*Spectacular achievement
is always preceded by
unspectacular preparation.*

Robert H. Schuller

# Day 16 Brainstorm Your Book Idea

*Give me six hours to chop down a tree and I will spend the first four sharpening the axe.*

Abraham Lincoln

After spending three weeks preparing, we are ready for take-off. It was necessary to ensure that our mindset, the environment, and the necessary tools are in place for the journey.

When you set out to become an author, you had an idea of what you'd write about. However, at this point, you need to eliminate any trace of vagueness in your idea. You also need to be clear about why anyone should read your book. Many books have been written, why is your yours different? Why should a reader pick yours out from a stack of books from a digital or physical platform? Here are ways to help you take-off.

## Determine your category

The two broad book categories are fiction and non-fiction. Book ideas in the fiction category are as vast as there are people and experiences. The major reason for writing fiction books is to provide a source of entertainment for your audience. However, fiction books are also the means through which many authors inspire their audiences.

In contrast, non-fiction books require that you write on facts. These have sub-categories such as inspiration, history, religion, etc. Choose both your category and sub-category and then move on to your specific idea. Even a rough idea of what you want to write about will make it easy to select your category and sub-category.

## Make your idea unique

As an author, it helps when you're aware of the information that's available out there. Just like you would do in the world of academia, you need to be clear about the unique perspective you are offering. Reading other books in your subject matter, for instance, will help you identify any existing information gaps that you could fill. Here are some pointers that could help you determine your book idea.

## Passion

What are you passionate about? What can you do for free all year long? If you can write on an idea that you are passionate about, you can be sure that you won't struggle along the way. If anything, you will be looking forward to your writing time. This is because you already have an internal drive towards the specific subject. This will be the proverbial killing of two birds with one stone. Not only will you enjoy the writing, you'll also get to become more proficient in your area of passion as you carry out your research.

## Experiences

Your life experiences are unique. Capitalising on them will help you develop your distinct book idea. You could choose a specific experience or choose to write your life story. Don't despise yourself. There are many life lessons you probably have learnt that only you can explain. On the other hand, you could choose one aspect of your life, such as friendships, career, marriage, or work-life balance and write on that.

## Strengths or weaknesses you overcame

There are things you do easily, and there are those you have struggled with but have overcome. Your book idea could center on either of these. Some of the most inspirational books are those where the author shares how they overcame a weakness, because audiences are able to identify with the author at the beginning of their journey. It also assures the reader that he or she can succeed in the same way.

## Perspective

Although there is nothing new under the sun, you have an inimitable outlook on certain life issues. Like we've already discussed, your unique perspective on what has already been written is a good book idea. For example, if you have parenting experience, or have worked with children with special needs, you can write about it.

- What else can you add to the list to help you come up with a unique book idea?

- If someone asked you what they should write about, which questions would you use to help them come up with a good idea?

Share your reflections with a partner or a writer's group.

This will help you explore other potential areas of interest you might go with. There's nothing wrong with having more than one book idea. All you need to do is prioritise them. Who knows, you may end up writing two or more books in the end!

## Writing Checklist

**Did I...**

- [ ] Read Day 16 Insights
- [ ] Write my reflection from today's reading
- [ ] Write my action plan
- [ ] Share my action plan for accountability with a partner or a writer's group

 # Think of Your Audience

*It's not about selling. It's about creating value for your audience.*

Jerry Allocca

Knowing whom you are writing for is crucial when starting the writing process. Your audience will influence everything else in the process, from the language used to the choice of editor, the design type, and the marketing and distribution avenues.

As you prepare to write, ask yourself these questions:

- Who is my audience?

- Where is my audience found?

- What is my audience interested in?

- What value can I add to my audience?

Once you are clear on your book idea, you also need to be aware of what your audience is looking for. This will go a long way in helping your book to sell. Find out where there is an intersection between what your readers love reading and what you plan to write about. This means you need to study your readers' major interests. This may sound like an uphill task, but there is a way out.

## Go online

There are many online platforms that sell books, or through which people can access eBooks. Amazon is one among many. Your book idea category comes in handy at this point. On the selected website, go to your category of books and select the ones that have a 5-star rating. Then, go over the reviews written by the customers.

Another approach for this is to check the books with the highest sales within your category. Read the reviews written by customers. What suggestions did they give? What did they like about the book? Note that and then move on to the next, and so on.

On the other hand, look at the books that have a 1-star rating. Find out why they got such a bad review. What did the customers complain about? What did they indicate as their reason for disappointment with the book? Did they give suggestions for improvement? Also, look for the books in your desired category that haven't sold. Try to find out why they didn't do well.

# Ask your people

Do a simple survey among your family members, relatives, and friends. Ask about their favourite books in your category. Ask them why they loved the book. You could also ask them what they would have loved to see written about in that specific category. Alternatively, ask them what topics they wish would be tackled.

Apart from family and friends, maximise on your networks. If you are planning to write a parenting book, liaise with fellow parents and ask them to share the survey with their social networks. If you are going to write about careers, look for young people or one person with a large network. Ask them to help you in this process.

## *How do you do this?*

1.  You might consider using Google Forms. The beauty with Google Forms is that you receive responses as they come. You also don't need to spend a coin printing out and distributing questionnaires. Just ensure your survey isn't too long, so that your respondents don't get bored.

2.  Other online tools you can use to do your survey include Survey Monkey or Questionpro.com.

3.  You can also visit www.answerthepublic.com where you can see the common questions that people ask concerning your topic of interest.

4.  Consolidate Your Findings

Once you have gathered your findings, make valid conclusions. Of course, you can't expect to meet everyone's expectations. You also can't ignore the facts. All you need to be clear about is where your audience's interests and your book idea meet.

Try to be as creative as you possibly can be for this. You may not meet 100% of what they want, but your way of presenting the information could hook them into buying the book. That's part of the reason why you need to get a captivating title, as we shall discuss later.

- In your book category of interest, what are some of the books you have read and loved? Why did you like them?

- In the same category, have you come across books you felt didn't meet your expectations? In what ways did you feel they were lacking?

- In what other ways can you establish the interests of your audience?

Remember to have realistic expectations when thinking about your audience. You won't make everyone happy, but you can aim at meeting their general needs or interests.

## Writing Checklist

**Did I...**

- [ ] Read Day 17 notes
- [ ] Write my reflection from today's reading
- [ ] Write my action plan
- [ ] Share my action plan for accountability with a partner or a writer's group

# Develop a Working Title for Your Book

*A good title is the title of a successful book.*

Raymond Chandler

As you begin the process of writing your manuscript, your working title is more than just a convenient way to refer to your book. A judiciously chosen title helps you stay focused and generates enthusiasm. At the same time, it helps convince a publisher and your target audience that your book is worth their investment.

You will probably revise and tweak your working title as you progress, and your editor or publisher may suggest some revisions. Nevertheless, it is worth investing time and creative energy in selecting a good working title now.

Some books have very long, expository titles. Others have very short, catchy or clever titles. Many books use a combination of short titles and elaborative subtitles.

With a solid book idea and an understanding of what your audience is looking for, you'll do yourself a favour by coming up with a captivating title. Why? Because it's a big part of the first impression prospective buyers of your book will have. As such, you need to start thinking about it as early as possible.

The good news is, this doesn't have to be your final title. Plus, you can have more than one working title. These are meant to help consolidate the main idea of your book. It is advisable to pick a working title that is unforgettable and is going to capture your readers' attention. You could also opt for a subtitle, which offers some more detail on the title. Whether you are writing a fiction or non-fiction book, ensure the working title suits the genre you have chosen.

## The Main Thing

Ideally, your working title needs to be closely related to the main message of the book. For example, although there are many chapters in an English text book for elementary school, they are all not suitable for all levels of learning. For instance, the title could be *Marriage* and perhaps the subtitle would be *Communicating with Your Partner*.

In the same way, your main idea could guide your choice of title. You may also choose to use a captivating question which your readers would be interested in.

## For Inspiration

If you are feeling absolutely stuck, don't worry. You can always fish around for ideas. One of the go-to places where you can view a large collection of books at no charge is Amazon. Look at the various categories and the related book titles. Which ones stand out? Which ones caught your attention? Better still, which ones are selling like hot cake? What do you find peculiar about their titles?

## Think About It

Perhaps answering the following questions might help you develop some possible book title ideas:

1.  What is the one thing I want my readers to take from the book?

2.  What is the perspective my book gives on the subject?

3.  What is the main subject of my book?

4.  What question does my book answer?

5.  What problem does my book tackle?

6.  How does my book differ from others on the same subject?

7.  How can I make the title worth remembering?

Keep in mind that the titles you select now don't have to be the final ones. They are only meant to guide you as you write. You have the freedom to change as you work along. You can also get ideas from some of the people who are close to you who will give you honest feedback. Whatever you do, have a working title to keep you on track.

- What other places or websites might you visit to check out some captivating book titles?

- Apart from books, are there other publications with attractive titles? What do you think makes them catchy?

- What TV programs or movie titles do you find interesting? Are there some that have great content but poor titles? Or are there some with great titles and poor content? What are your reasons for these conclusions?

Share your reflections with a partner or a writer's group.

## Writing Checklist

**Did I...**

- [ ] Read Day 18 Insights
- [ ] Write my reflection from today's reading
- [ ] Write my action plan
- [ ] Share my action plan for accountability with a partner or a writer's group

# Create a Book Mind Map

*Normal linear note taking and writing will put you into a semi-hypnotic trance, while mind mapping will greatly enhance your left and right brain cognitive skills.*

Tony Buzan

Have you ever heard of a mind map?

A mind map is a tool for the brain that captures the thinking that goes on inside your head. Mind mapping helps you think, collect knowledge, remember, and create ideas. Most likely it will make you a better thinker.

A central theme is placed in the centre of a blank page. This is the title, the subject, a problem or just a thought.

From the central theme, associations radiate out. Associations that are directly from the central theme are called first-level associations. Second-level associations are then created, then third-level and so on. The brain thinks by imagination and association. When associations are created, connections are made. These connections are essential for remembering and thinking.

What comes to your mind when you think of a map? Isn't it a reference point that allows you to get direction to a place? In most cases, there's always a starting point and the desired destination. From the map, you get to determine the possible routes you can use and eventually, you pick the one that is most convenient.

In the same way, your book mind map will help you to draw the connections between related ideas. This will help you consolidate your thoughts in an orderly manner and avoid repeating yourself. Here, you don't have to be neat. Just jot down all your ideas and see which ones relate to each other.

# Centre Your Working Title

Your mind map helps you glance at your entire book in pictorial form. You can liken it to a pictograph that captures all the info in an article. This follows the principle that a picture is worth a million words.

The title should be right in the middle of your map. The rest of the ideas should stem from this title. It is also important to ensure that the ideas are not so far-removed from the title(s) you have chosen. That way, each idea will build up towards the main idea of the book.

# Encircle the Sub-themes

What are the building blocks you'll need to pass the message across? Ideally, they should be related to the working title of your book. You may not exhaust these at once, but put down the ones that come to mind immediately. Then you can always add to them as you go.

You may want to put big circles or boxes around these sub-themes. Leave enough space to add the details we'll talk about next. You can also use sticky notes if you find that more interesting. The idea is to ensure there is a visible arrangement of thought.

# Populate the Sub-theme Boxes or Circles

Within each of the spaces left for the sub-themes, write out the ideas you'll use to capture the entire thought. To get several ideas in each sub-theme, consider breaking down your sub-theme into smaller categories. Then think of the details that you cannot afford to miss out on to communicate your message in detail.

*Example:*

Say your working title is Clothing Trends in 2020. Your sub-themes could be beach attire, official wear, casual wear, sports wear and smart casual. Then under each sub-theme, you'll break down the different combinations of clothes/ colors, tops/bottoms, shoes/ hats etc.

Some mind map platforms include Xmind - and Lucidchart.

Finally, you can begin to consider which sub-theme should go first, second, third, and so forth. This will help you to finally draw your book outline, as we shall see later.

- What do you think is the most convenient place to draw your book mind map (on paper, laptop, tablet, other option)? Why do you think so?

- Where can you get more ideas for your book mind map?

- What are the challenges you might face while creating your book mind map?

Share your reflections with a partner or a writer's group.

Find out how to overcome your challenges.

Whatever you do, don't stop moving forward. You've made it this far.

## Writing Checklist

**Did I...**

- [ ] Read Day 19 Insights
- [ ] Write my reflection from today's reading
- [ ] Write my action plan
- [ ] Share my action plan for accountability with a partner or a writer's group

<table>
<tr><td>Day 20</td><td>

# Develop an Outline for Your Book
</td></tr>
</table>

*I always work from an outline, so I know all the of the broad events and some of the finer details before I begin writing the book*

Mercedes Lackey

With your book mind map done, your next step is to convert it to a book outline.

Your book outline provides you with the structure of your book. If you start writing without a good outline, you risk taking forever or not finishing your book at all. Your book is also likely to be haphazard and incomplete.

A book outline is your best guard against fear, anxiety, procrastination, and writer's block. With clarity on the audience and a good outline, the actual writing of the book becomes fairly easy as you will discover. The basic idea is to use the book outline as a roadmap to help you know what to write in each chapter.

With your book mind map in place, you can now develop the outline of your book. An outline functions like the blueprint of a building. It is drawn to give a guideline on how to construct, the time limit for it, and the order to be followed throughout the construction process. Similarly, your book outline will help you determine what you'll need to write about and how it should be arranged chronologically.

Perhaps understanding the importance of an outline may motivate you to develop one for yourself before you start writing. Here are some of the advantages of writing a book outline:

## Helps you write faster

You won't be wondering what to write about, since you have already thought of this before you start writing.

## Clarifies your goals

With an outline, you'll know exactly what you plan to put down and why. This clarity prevents you from going round in circles and or ending up on dead ends.

## Maintains your focus

The outline of your book will ensure you don't take a tangent that leads away from what you had set out to write about from the onset.

## Generates a working plan

With an outline, you can easily determine how to write each chapter, and what to tackle each day and week. In fact, with an outline, you can tell how long it'll take to write your book and set a realistic deadline. It also gives you a chronological overview of the book.

You'll be able to see the end of your book before you begin writing and have a concrete plan on how your thoughts will follow each other. Your mind will find it easier to work with this pre-determined pattern.

## Facilitates changes

It is much easier to play around with the arrangement of the outline than shift entire chapters.

*How do you develop the outline?*

If you had the book mind map, developing the outline shouldn't be difficult. You may notice that some of the ideas you came up with may not meet the objective of your book. It may be best to discard them (or possibly keep them aside for another book).

Afterwards, transform each sub-theme in your book mind map into a chapter. Then you can go ahead and create a new book mind map for each of the chapters. This will depend heavily on the key ideas you had allocated to the sub-themes. Avoid being too detailed at this point though.

After this, determine the chronological order of the chapters. Don't forget to include the introduction and the conclusion of the book. With these, you're good to go!

How do you intend to create your book outline?

If you were to present a report about everything you've learnt on your book-writing journey thus far, how would you prepare your presentation? Think of this report as your book and create the outline.

Share your reflections with a partner or a writer's group.

## Writing Checklist

**Did I...**

- [ ] Read Day 20 Insights
- [ ] Write my reflection from today's reading
- [ ] Write my action plan
- [ ] Share my action plan for accountability with a partner or a writer's group

# THE WRITER'S JOURNEY

*The journey of a thousand miles begins with one step.*

Lao Tzu

# Day 21  Write Your First Chapter

*[As a writer] you have to have the three D's: drive, discipline, and desire. If you're missing any one of those three, you can have all the talent in the world, but it's going to be really hard to get anything done.*

Nora Roberts

*You have to follow your own voice. You have to be yourself when you write. In effect, you have to announce, 'This is me, this is what I stand for, this is what you get when you read me. I'm doing the best I can—buy me or not—but this is who I am as a writer.*

David Morrell

Armed with your book mind map and outline, you have an opportunity to start your writing journey today. Whether you complete the chapter in one seating is not the issue, it is the discipline that matters. Keep writing.

You've come this far and probably already have your book outline in place.Congratulations! Now all you need to do is start writing chapter one. Once you get this chapter done, you'll easily write the rest. The good news is that you already know how to do this the right way.

Refer to your book mind map and outline. Refresh your mind on the ideas you were to tackle in chapter 1. You may want to zoom in on the chapter and create a specific mind map for it. From the ideas in the book mind map, develop the content of your chapter. Include all the relevant research you have gathered on the content.

Arrange the ideas in a logically coherent way. Ensure the ideas are flowing smoothly. Then you can set out to flesh out your chapter. There are several ways to do this:

## Writing

The most obvious way to do this is by using your chosen writing tool. Go to your writing space, switch on your laptop or tablet and begin writing. You'll refer to the chapter mind map severally as you write it out. Remember to stick to the time you blocked out for writing. Avoid all distractions and write away.

# Speaking

Another way to develop your first chapter is to record yourself as you speak on the ideas you have outlined. This works for certain people who just love the idea of hearing their thoughts out loud. Feel free to record your thoughts in whatever way you want. Just be sure you name the recording appropriately.

Afterwards, write down whatever you recorded. You'll make faster progress with an audio recording than having to write without one. In fact, if your outline is ready and has all the details you want to include in your book, there's a possibility of speaking your entire book within 3 hours! This is likely to motivate you to finish your book even faster since you already have the content in audio form.

The best part of this method is that if you notice any problems with the flow of the story while writing, you can correct as you go, thus eliminating major errors as you continue writing. However, this doesn't guarantee you an error-free manuscript. It will still need to go through the editing and proofreading process so that it is ready for publication.

Even so, speaking your book content first before writing it is bound to shorten your writing time. You'll have your entire chapter and book ready by your deadline date.

**It's time to reflect!**

- How can you ensure you meet your daily writing targets?

- Do you think speaking your book will work better for you, or do you prefer writing it out? Give reasons for your choice.

- Would you rather write out your spoken content or have someone else do it for you? Why?

Share your reflections with a partner or a writer's group.

Remember to celebrate this milestone!

## Writing Checklist

**Did I...**

- [ ] Read Day 21 Insights
- [ ] Write my reflection from today's reading
- [ ] Write my action plan
- [ ] Share my action plan for accountability with a partner or a writer's group

# KEEP WRITING

*"Doing it all the time, whether or not we are in the mood, gives us ownership of our writing ability. It takes it out of the realm of conjuring where we stand on the rock of isolation, begging the winds for inspiration, and it makes it something as doable as picking up a hammer and pounding a nail. Writing may be an art, but it is certainly a craft. It is a simple and workable thing that can be as steady and reliable as a chore."*

Julia Cameron

The idea to book challenge was merely the kick-off for your book-writing initiative. You need to keep writing and move forward. A few reminders for a successful writing journey is that you need:

- **A writing community** – If you are interested, you will be invited to join a **Writers' Support Group** that will allow sharing of tools and resources as well as ideas to help overcome some of the identified challenges in both the writing process and content development.

- **Accountability** – Having an accountability partner is very helpful. I would encourage you to go the extra mile and remain engaged to fully reap the benefits of all the efforts that went into this ambitious exercise. I am sure this will be a worthwhile effort as we heard that many participants are eager to use the principles to inform their writing.

# REFERENCES & RESOURCES

1.  Chandler Bolt. (2019, October 20). How to write a book step by step: With a free book template. Self Publishing School. https://self-publishingschool.com/how-to-write-a-book/

2.  (n.d.). MindMup. https://www.mindmup.com/

3.  (2020, June 22). Popplet | Mind maps made easy. https://popplet.com/

4.  The scribe blog: Written by a 4x NY times Bestselling author. (2018, April 28). Scribe Writing. https://scribewriting.com/blog/5. Smith, G. (2013, September 25). 24 essential mind mapping and brainstorming tools. Mashable. https://mashable.com/2013/09/25/mind-mapping-tools/

# About the Author

Kirimi Barine has been involved in training, publishing, and coaching for more than two decades with the intention of inspiring lives and transforming people for productivity, performance, as well as rapid and effective results. Dr Barine has earned the ATD Master Trainer™ designation for train the trainercoaching and training delivery.

He holds a PhD in Business Administration with a bias in leadership and governance, a Master's in Business Administration, and a Bachelor of Education degree. Barine was formerly the Publisher and CEO at Evangel Publishing House. He currently coordinates publishing development at the United Bible Societies.

Dr Barine is an author and co-author of several books, among them Transformational Corporate Leadership and African Christian Leadership: Realities, Opportunities and Impact.

www.kirimi-barine.com

# BOOKS BY THE AUTHOR

www.ingramcontent.com/pod-product-compliance
Lightning Source LLC
Chambersburg PA
CBHW020127180726
47992CB00020B/2532